WORDS FOR MY DAUGHTER

THE NATIONAL POETRY SERIES

The National Poetry Series was established in 1978 to ensure the publication of five books of poetry each year through a series of participating publishers. Each manuscript is selected by a poet of national reputation. Publication is funded by the Copernicus Society of America, James A. Michener, Edward J. Piszek, and The Lannan Foundation.

1990 PUBLICATIONS

WORDS FOR MY DAUGHTER, by John Balaban
Selected by W.S. Merwin. Copper Canyon Press.

QUESTIONS ABOUT ANGELS, by Billy Collins
Selected by Edward Hirsch. William Morrow & Co.

THE ISLAND ITSELF, by Roger Fanning
Selected by Michael Ryan. The Viking Press.

RAINBOW REMNANTS IN ROCK BOTTOM GHETTO SKY,
by Thylias Moss
Selected by Charles Simic. Persea Books.

THE SURFACE, by Laura Mullen
Selected by C.K. Williams. University of Illinois Press.

OTHER BOOKS BY JOHN BALABAN

POETRY

AFTER OUR WAR (University of Pittsburgh Press, 1974) Lamont Award

BLUE MOUNTAIN (Unicorn Press, 1982)

TRANSLATION

CA DAO VIETNAM: A BILINGUAL ANTHOLOGY
OF VIETNAMESE FOLK POETRY (Unicorn Press, 1974)

NONFICTION

VIETNAM: THE LAND WE NEVER KNEW (Chronicle Books, 1989)

REMEMBERING HEAVEN'S FACE (Simon & Schuster/Poseidon, 1991)

FICTION

COMING DOWN AGAIN (Simon & Schuster/Fireside, 1989)

THE HAWK'S TALE (Harcourt Brace Jovanovich, 1988)

WORDS FOR MY DAUGHTER

POEMS BY

JOHN BALABAN

COPPER CANYON PRESS
PORT TOWNSEND

ACKNOWLEDGMENTS: Some of these poems have appeared in *Blue Mountain,*
Harper's, Ploughshares, Triquarterly, Poet Lore, The Poetry Review, New England Review,
Prairie Schooner and *Ms. Magazine.*

Copper Canyon Press is in residence with Centrum at Fort Worden State Park.

COPPER CANYON PRESS

P.O. Box 271, Port Townsend, Washington   98368

For Tally

CONTENTS

PART ONE

Words for My Daughter

About eight of us were nailing up forts
in the mulberry grove behind Reds's house
when his mother started screeching and
all of us froze except Reds — fourteen, huge
as a hippo — who sprang out of the tree so fast
the branch nearly bobbed me off. So fast,
he hit the ground running, hammer in hand,
and seconds after he got in the house
we heard thumps like someone beating a tire
off a rim   his dad's howls the screen door
banging open   Saw   Reds barreling out
through the tall weeds towards the highway
the father stumbling after his fat son
who never looked back across the thick swale
of teazel and black-eyed susans until it was safe
to yell fuck you at the skinny drunk
stamping around barefoot and holding his ribs.

Another time, the Connelly kid came home to find
his alcoholic mother getting raped by the milkman.
Bobby broke a milkbottle and jabbed the guy
humping on his mom. I think it really happened
because none of us would loosely mention that

wraith of a woman who slippered around her house
and never talked to anyone, not even her kids.
Once a girl ran past my porch
with a dart in her back, her open mouth
pumping like a guppy's, her eyes wild.
Later that summer, or maybe the next,
the kids hung her brother from an oak.
Before they hoisted him, yowling and heavy
on the clothesline, they made him claw the creekbank
and eat worms. I don't know why his neck didn't snap.

Reds had another nickname you couldn't say
or he'd beat you up: "Honeybun."
His dad called him that when Reds was little.

                    *

So, these were my playmates. I love them still
for their justice and valor and desperate loves
twisted in shapes of hammer and shard.
I want you to know about their pain
and about the pain they could loose on others.
If you're reading this, I hope you will think,
Well, my Dad had it rough as a kid, so what?
If you're reading this, you can read the news
and you know that children suffer worse.

                    *

Worse for me is a cloud of memories
still drifting off the South China Sea,
like the 9-year-old boy, naked and lacerated,
thrashing in his pee on a steel operating table
and yelling *"Dau. Dau,"* while I, trying to translate
in the mayhem of Tet for surgeons who didn't know
who this boy was or what happened to him, kept asking
"Where? Where's the pain?" until a surgeon
said "Forget it. His ears are blown."

*

I remember your first Hallowe'en
when I held you on my chest and rocked you,
so small your toes didn't touch my lap
as I smelled your fragrant peony head
and cried because I was so happy and because
I heard, in no metaphorical way, the awful chorus
of Soeur Anicet's orphans writhing in their cribs.
Then the doorbell rang and a tiny Green Beret
was saying trick-or-treat and I thought *oh oh*
but remembered it was Hallowe'en and where I was.
I smiled at the evil midget, his map-light and night
paint, his toy knife for slitting throats, said,
"How ya doin', soldier?" and, still holding you asleep
in my arms, gave him a Mars Bar. To his father
waiting outside in fatigues I hissed, "You shit,"
and saw us, child, in a pose I know too well.

I want you to know the worst and be free from it.
I want you to know the worst and still find good.
Day by day, as you play nearby or laugh
with the ladies at Peoples Bank as we go around town
and I find myself beaming like a fool,
I suspect I am here less for your protection
than you are here for mine, as if you were sent
to call me back into our helpless tribe.

Heading Out West

All evening, below a sprig of yarrow,
by creekwater plunging through willow roots,
a cricket preened its song in our yard.

Down by the back eddy spinning with whirligigs,
I watched a fox pause from lapping up water
to lift a delicate paw and scratch
at redmites itching the root of its ear.

Then, as the sun ignited the willow stand
a blackbird flapped off a branch,
crossing shadowy fields like a thought.

All evening as crickets called, I creaked
a rocker on our paint-peeled porch,
sipped whisky, watched mist and fireflies
fill up the meadow, and considered
—long before I was a father—
my fellow Americans, the funny business of being married,
my deadly job and the jobs that would follow,
and all I could think of as I sat there

−safe from harm, steadily employed, happily married−
was how to get away.

                At morning, I left,
hopping a ride west on the interstate, past
the cauldrons of Pittsburgh, its choked air,
past HoJos, Exxons, Arbys, Gulfs,
in the yammer and slam, the drone of trucks,
past the little lives that always are there,
past locusts chirring in a Tennessee graveyard,
past kudzu, pecans, then yucca and sage,
past armadillos scuttling off the berm of the highway,
. . . all the while wondering just what I was doing,
not sure where I was going; less sure, why.
But standing there, hanging out my thumb,
squinting at the stream of oncoming cars.

Daddy Out Hitchhiking at 3:00 A.M.

Finally it was just me, and the katydids
cranking out nightsongs in clumps of willows
by a barn roofed in moonlight, by a ryefield
luminous with dew. I stepped off the highway
ribboning out through the valley. Walked
through wet weeds to a pond gathering vapors.

Angels see the way I saw that night
when only large shapes loomed
and all my thoughts were laid aside
as I searched the night opening before me
and soul shuffled out of self to sing
with katydids chattering in murky trees.

All beasts are kind with divine instruction.
The paired ducks slept beneath their wings.
Minnows wavered in the moon-charmed creek
where a muskrat hunched and licked its paws
listening like me to insects calling
searching and calling at the end of summer.

This is what Daddy was doing
the August you were born.
Wandering off alone on highways
walking off highways into the night
calming a head loud with the past
listening to things that make a song.

Crossing West Nebraska,
Looking for Blue Mountain

Where can one find the real Blue Mountain?
Inside the Blue Mountain at Waggoner's Gap,
is there another, pulsing cool azure light?
Can one drive west and find Blue Mountain?
Will anyone ever live there but me?
Some say that Blue Mountain is very small
and is rocking in the zion of a waterbead.
They claim to find it everywhere, even in clouds
of atmospheric dust snapping with strontium
and settling on the grasslands this evening.
Although Blue Mountain is only as large as a thought,
its sides drop off into dark crags; its steep slopes
are smooth as glass; its aspect is discouraging.
But from its peak, one can see everything clearly:

In humming fields, beetles, aphids, weevils, ants.
Fox pups frisking in bluebells before their burrow.
A naked boy and girl dogpaddling an inner tube
in bayou waters, off a levee near Big Mamou.
Subterranean rocks grinding in the San Andreas Fault.
A Malay fisherman, perched on a spit of rock off Penang,
hurling a circling net into surf at sunset.
A bloated mare giving foal in a clover field in Kent.
A blindfolded teenager, shoeless, slumped against a tree

as the firing squad walks off in Montevideo.
Missiles hidden like moles in Siberian silos.
A black man, in red cotton shirt and khaki pants, his skin
alive with protozoan welts, sipping coffee in a Congo shop.
An eel sliding through a corpse's yellowed ribs
in a Mekong swamp where frogs croak and egrets fish.
Ice sparkling the coats of hundreds of reindeer with
steaming nostrils, crossing a Lapland river under a moon.

As I pass in the dark through this sleeping town
the only creatures moving on Main Street are moths.
Spinning orbits about the lamps, they fall and die.
Their husks rustle like leaves in the fluorescent light.
Were they flying to Blue Mountain? Am I there?

Riding Westward

"Hence is't, that I am carryed towards the West
This day, when my Soules forme bends towards the East."
— JOHN DONNE, "Goodfriday, 1613. Riding Westward"

You know that something's not quite right.
Perhaps the town is one of those
which marks its name and elevation
on a water tower stuck up on a hill.
Or maybe the hill itself declares the name
in whitewashed stones set just behind the town.
The big thing is the grain elevators.
The blacktop runs straight into them
just as country roads point to steeples
in Protestant towns along the Rhine.
But these tall towers are filled with wheat,
with corn and oats and rye, not hymns
to the stern father who sends us to the fields
or bids us read his Book before we eat,
who shuts our eyes in calms of beast-like sleep.

This poem is no tract for Jesus.
No fewer evils or epiphanies of joy
rise up here than did in Europe, which these
good farmers left because it was a grave.
Still one wonders. What was all this for,
the grizzled duffer in the John Deere cap asks
as he shuffles to Main Street's secondhand sale.
Rubble of shoes in cardboard boxes. And boots,

old button boots, a pile of iron peaveys
which rolled cottonwoods down from the river,
the forest long since cleared. Cracked photos
of a jackrabbit hunt, the creatures piled high
in heaps before the log-and-sod schoolhouse.

I mean, he asks, as he tweaks his balls
through the hole in his right jean pocket,
why did they do this? What was it for?
The doves perch on a wire above the dusty road.
Swallows sweep into a storefront eave.
A clump of orange lilies closes with the day.
A CB chatters in a parked Ford truck
its back-bed loaded up with bales of hay:
"We got a Kojak with a Kodak takin' pictures
... he done a flipflop on the superslab."
The pickup's empty; the owner's in the bar.

The rightest place to worry this thing out
is at the first dead farmhouse outside town.
Sit there on the stoop's blistered boards
as swallows chitter towards their roosts,
the fat sun sinking in reddish pollen haze
beyond the silos, beyond the tassled fields.

Passing Through Albuquerque

At dusk, by the irrigation ditch
gurgling past backyards near the highway,
locusts raise a maze of calls in cottonwoods.

A Spanish girl in a white party dress
strolls the levee by the muddy water
where her small sister plunks in stones.

Beyond a low adobe wall and a wrecked car
men are pitching horseshoes in a dusty lot.
Someone shouts as he clangs in a ringer.

Big winds buffet in ahead of a storm,
rocking the immense trees and whipping up
clouds of dust, wild leaves, and cottonwool.

In the moment when the locusts pause and the girl
presses her up-fluttering dress to her bony knees
you can hear a banjo, guitar, and fiddle

playing "The Mississippi Sawyer" inside a shack.
Moments like that, you can love this country.

Agua Fria y Las Chicharras

I: ALHAMBRA

When the voice of the Prophet crossed the Sahara
clattering out from mud-walled souks with Berber horsemen,
it carried swiftly through those wastes, for as the Arabs say,
in the desert there is nothing but the presence of Allah.
And in Granada, below snow peaks rinsing in sunlight,
at the Alhambra, Al Qal'a al-Hamara, the Architect's Garden,
the Moors made Him visible everywhere, in horseshoe portals
and sandstone ramparts stamped with the Key,
in icy fountains teased out from the rock
looping towards heaven, collapsing in pools, plunging down
stairwells banistered in liquid light. *Quien quiere agua?*
the water-carriers sang, *agua mas fria que nieve.*
In the spill of water, the signature of god.
And outside the citadel of Allah, in paradisiacal parks,
the locusts calling at the edge of wilderness.

II: ARROYO HONDO, NEW MEXICO

He pitched his camp inside a canyon
where willows twist on boulders shoved up beside the creek.
Poplars shook out sunlight after a rain. By the dead fire
lay a charred bean can and a plastic bag spilling out flour.

In the creek, a Coors six-pack; a pint of half-and-half.
He had some clothes draping a rock, a bedroll
sprawled on soggy blankets. By that, an empty suitcase.
I found him staring at the stream.
He looked about thirty, said he lived near Denver,
put up sheetrock for a living, was leaving for L.A.
He said he had been to her place in town. It was empty.
He stood outside her house until he heard echoes gather,
saw shapes move, imagined her children's yelps,
her laughter, her husband's arms around her
as they leaned against the sink and kissed.
The marigolds she left behind still glimmered in the shade
below the cottonwood where, high up, locusts called.
He said it was like he saw her reading by the window
then putting down the book to stare at him staring in.
Like a ghost watching a ghost. He offered me a beer
saying he had come here through a valley of lies
with no guide but hunger for her. No Christ, no cop, no book,
no mother or father, no flag, and the few friends he counted
were gone and God knows where. She too was gone for good.
He wanted me to know about a lake,
dry, some sixty miles up north in Colorado
where Indians emerged as men, led out, led up
from Sipapu, the Underworld, upon pulses of song
by Kokopelli, The Hump-Backed Flute Player, the Locust God,
whose song can heal. We sipped his beer and listened
to whines of locusts falling on the creek.

III: Rosale's

Ro-*sah*-le's. Just north of Taos in El Prado
past the feed sign for henscratch: $5.50/50 lbs.
You go there if you're hungry and it's late.
Rosale's a Mexican from Juarez, does a big business
from midnight to dawn when all the drunks
and lounge lizards stumble in as bars shut down.

So everyone's ugly and stiff in the eye sockets
because it's too late to get laid, because
their lives stink. So they fight.
Once the cops raided and took away a lot of guns
but I never heard of anyone *dying* there
so I go . . . and one night I saw an awful fight
with four drunks kicking this squirmy Anglo
who had been cold-cocked while eating his eggs
and lay groaning below a table, everyone just watching
until the big girl in the blue smock waddled out
from the kitchen, screamed, and shoved them out.
No fun in that fight at all.

When I left, dawn was cracking behind the mountains
and high up I saw the bright porpoise brow of a jet
streaming east, nose silvery with sunlight
above the darkened earth. The plane was a comfort
darting across the open sky like a clear thought,

it said, "Look around. The signs are all about you
even in a sorry brawl in a Mexican cafe."
Each spring, I thought, they clean the ditches,
the *aquecias*, of leaf muck and debris.
Each must marvel when waters spill again
and cottonwoods shimmer in a web of poems
as redwings bob and whistle the branches
and canyons fill with the locusts' song.
Oh, the hunger for words pure as clear water
that will slake the pain of our parched tongues
and, splashed against our brows, shall let us see.
In such a moment, locusts reinstruct our rapture.
Cold and mute, we are led up from dark worlds
into a sunstruck glade loud with rilling water.
At the song's start, the raw tongue stammers out
an urge towards paradise, a version of ease.

Lovers Near Jemez Springs

Across the canyon creek
bridged with bubbled ice
snow filled their tracks

through aspens
up the whitening hill
along the power line path

falling, filling their footprints
where they halted by the doe
stretched stiff in the snow

where they worked on
through dusted blackberry canes
into hushed pines

to the cattle pond
drained by muskrats
and sprouting dead cattails

where her footsteps
went to the snow-drifted bank
and his scuffed the glaze

over the pond's heart
as they talked. Snow filled
their footsteps where they came together.

*

Spring in these woods
is all fern swale, teaberry,
Indian pipes and paintbrush

. the doe, a dried rug
on a rack of bones,
the brambles; flowering.

The pond rustles green sheaves
as red-wings bob
in wild alfalfa

and peepers keen the bog.
All this occurs without her.
He comes here alone.

And where leaves unfurl
from oak and cottonwood,
he sees instead a snowfall.

And where chokecherry shakes
in tiny blossoms,
he sees a falling snow.

Snowbound

Tragedies of clouds still stumble over us
stalled in cars and tractor trailers
along the highway blocked at a mountain pass,
but now a track team from a chartered bus
has shoved a van past a jack-knifed trailer
and so, after long hours, a lane is cleared
for all the bickering parents and bratty kids
for truckers zonked on speed and nattering on CBs
for the long-hauler with straggly hair and no front teeth
who struck out in the snow to straighten things out
and who stomped back angry, for the snoozing salesmen,
for the old folks too shy to pee by the road
for the teenagers yelling in hormonal fits
for the wailing babies, for the diabetic
shooting his thigh behind a fogged windshield
for the lovers feeling lucky at being trapped together
and, oh, just wishing it were night
for all of us now inching forward in a glittering line
resuming our lives under a sweep of clearing sky.

Some Things That Happened Before My Daughter's Birth

---

1. A Poem Her Mother Wrote Me The Year I Was Away

Snow piles up these lonely nights.
This winter you are gone.
Knee-deep, February drifts choke
the railroad bed we walked in summer
edged by daisies and black-eyed susans.

From the woods Rangers drag out deer,
Ribs poke through their rusty coats.
The Rangers say "no food." Too much snow.
The coldest winter in our century.

Fitting that we should be apart.
Powerful winds and hibernation of the soul.
Like the deer pawing for bark, I peel away
the crust of my own heart, pumping these days
in a white expanse, frozen every dawn,
as snow falls where we walked together.

2. My Reply

"Sweetest love, I do not go
For weariness of thee...."
—John Donne

Let's say that I was called away
summoned by a voice I heard first as a boy
when belly down on the cool bank
I looked in the clattering water
at skeeters sculling tiny oars,
at a crayfish wading through willow roots
unraveling under clear ripples.
I was so still a woodthrush supped beside me.
So quiet, I dwelt with spotted newts.

"Come" is all that voice has ever said,
wet with ferns and mossy logs
with catbird cry and frog croak.
And when I followed I was always happy
reading delight in signatures of fish,
in moth glyphs scribbled beneath elm bark,
even though lonely; as now, for you.

What calls me away shall call me home.
I knew your voice before we met.
These journeys out, are journeys back.
Let's say my travels tend towards you.

Thoughts Before Dawn

(for Mary Bui Thi Khuy, 1944-1969)

The bare oaks rock and snowcrust tumbles down.
The creaking eave woke me thinking of you
crushed by a truck thirteen years ago
when the drunk A RV N lost the wheel.

We brought to better care the nearly lost,
the boy burned by white phosphorus, chin
glued to his chest; the scalped girl;
the triple amputee from the road-mined bus;
the kid without a jaw; the one with no nose.
You never wept in front of them, but waited
until the gurney rolled them into surgery.
I guess that's what amazed me most.
Why didn't you fall apart or quit?

Once, we flew two patched kids home,
getting in by Army chopper,
a Huey Black Cat that skimmed the sea.
When the gunner opened up on a whale
you closed your eyes and covered your ears
and your small body shook in your silk *ao dai*.
Oh, Mary. In this arctic night, awake in my bed

I rehearse your smile, bright white teeth,
the funny way you rode your Honda 50, perched
so straight, silky hair bunned up in a brim hat,
front brim blown back, and dark glasses.
Brave woman, I hope you never saw the truck.

For the Missing In Action

Hazed with heat and harvest dust
the air swam with flying husks
as men whacked rice sheaves into bins
and all across the sunstruck fields
red flags hung from bamboo poles.
Beyond the last treeline on the horizon
beyond the coconut palms and eucalyptus
out in the moon zone puckered by bombs
the dead earth where no one ventures,
the boys found it, foolish boys
riding buffaloes in craterlands
where at night bombs thump and ghosts howl.
A green patch on the raw earth.
And now they've led the farmers here,
the kerchiefed women in baggy pants,
the men with sickles and flails, children
herding ducks with switches — all
staring from a crater berm; silent:
In that dead place the weeds had formed a man
where someone died and fertilized the earth, with flesh
and blood, with tears, with longing for loved ones.
No scrap remained; not even a buckle
survived the monsoons, just a green creature,

a viney man, supine, with posies for eyes,
butterflies for buttons, a lily for a tongue.
Now when huddled asleep together
the farmers hear a rustly footfall
as the leaf-man rises and stumbles to them.

The Water Buffalo

(Hanoi, 1972)

The rain drizzled and shifted
over rippling green fields of rice.
Every drop will grow a grain.

The lop-eared banana leaves
opened an umbrella over me
and I sank into an ancient hush.

An old man with a buffalo
stood at the end of the path.
Both were carved in wood.

Without a word the old man
parted a curtain of leaves
to let me into his house.

I stepped across the threshold
and froze before a gaping hole,
a crater bigger than a grave.

Smoke rose from ashes,
black smoke curling in the wind.
Dry wells, instead of walls.

My host slid down to the bottom,
calling me, with beckoning hand,
to his family in the pit.

His grandson – a tuft of hair,
His old woman – the handle of a pot,
His strapping sons – bloody stones.

His pretty girls – threads of cloth,
His sons-in-law – sandal thongs,
His daughters-in-law – lumps of earth.

His brother, on a visit – a broken stool,
His great-grandson, still in the womb
of his mother – a banana shoot.

The shoot, as if still growing,
had a green bud which resembled
the clenched fist of a baby.

. . . To have lived a long life honestly,
to have raised a big family
by yourself, and in your old age

to be left alone with your buffalo,
the only living creature
with whom to share your sorrow.

The inventions of America, those
gadgets, machines, technical wonders—
is this what they are for?

from the Bulgarian of Blaga Dimitrova

Atomic Ghost

As our plane droned south to Peoria
all the cattle ponds and creeks below
caught sun, flared bright, then faded
back into smog seeping from Chicago,
so that looking west through oval ports
you saw jags of water wink and flash.

Then the sky ballooned with light so bright
the firmament bucked and our plane
dropped like a long sigh through magnetized air
and the woman who ordered a Bloody Mary
swirled in her seat, a small cyclone of ash
saying syllables of smoke in the whirligig fire.

Almost at once, cells quirked and recombined.
In the company of scorched ant and armadillo
new lives shuffled forth, sick in their seed,
irradiated, wracked with lunatic genes.
Queer things issued from monsters of the past
as earth reassessed the error that was man,
that was me, my wife, our child. All
entered the pall of incinerated air.

Oh, to be cast from the Garden again and forever.

Mr. Giai's Poem

The French ships shelled Haiphong then took the port.
Mr. Giai was running down a road, mobilized,
with two friends, looking for their unit in towns
where thatch and geese lay shattered on the roads
and smoke looped up from cratered yards. A swarm
of bullock carts and bicycles streamed against them
as trousered women strained with children, chickens,
charcoal, and rice towards Hanoi in the barrage lull.
Then, Giai said, they saw just stragglers.
Ahead, the horizon thumped with bombs.

At an empty inn they tried their luck
though the waiter said he'd nothing left.
"Just a coffee,"said Mr. Giai. "A sip
of whisky," said one friend. "A cigarette," the other.
Miraculously, these each appeared. Serene,
they sat a while, then went to fight.
Giai wrote a poem about that pause for *Ve Quoc Quan*,
the Army paper. Critics found the piece bourgeois.

Forty years of combat now behind him
—Japanese, Americans, and French.
Wounded twice, deployed in jungles for nine years,
his son just killed in Kampuchea,

Giai tells this tale to three Americans
each young enough to be his son:
an ex-Marine once rocketed in Hue,
an Army grunt, mortared at Bong Son,
a CO hit by a stray of shrapnel,

all four now silent in the floating restaurant
rocking on moorlines in the Saigon river.
Crabshells and beer bottles litter their table.
A rat runs a rafter overhead. A wave slaps by.
"That moment," Giai adds, "was a little like now."
They raise their glasses to the river's amber light,
all four as quiet as if carved in ivory.

Chasing Out the Demons

(for Tim Buckley)

A bad case. Alone in the canyon,
screaming and charging a dirtbike
at the sandstone cliffs, he squinted
behind his wire-rim glasses
as the bugs splashed green and he bucked
across cottonwood roots and rubble
at breakneck speed, on a whining bike,
skidding to stops at the canyon walls.

At night, zipped in a sleeping bag,
he squirmed like a chrysalis under the moon
while the wind searched the willows
and the creek plunked into little pools
where trout batted at fireflies.

The two Indians came in his sleep:
two ghosts, pulses of wind and moonlight,
squatting beside him on the balls of their feet.
He shouted when the woman smoothed his hair.
And then they were gone and he cried.
Sobbed hard because it was goodbye,
goodbye to the spirit that raged in him by day
and now was traveling across the canyon creek

led off by the ghosts of two Indians
who had come to calm him.

He sat up that night by the dark cold water,
wrapped in a blanket, listening to the creek,
breaking his reverie only once
to cup his hands and draw to his lips
the moon rocking on the clear water.

Peyote Villanelle

"Watch out for this one, USA."
—PEYOTE ROAD CHIEF, Taos

1. The trail lost, he looked about
   across the bouldered canyon floor.
   In desert wastes the soul cries out

   then echoes back in dusty shouts,
   wavering ghosts in chaparral.
   The trail lost, he looked about

   the creekbed where he shot his mount.
   Horseflies sucked the splash of gore.
   In desert wastes the soul cries out.

   Though no one heard, he called out loud.
   Snakes uncurled in a cave's cool door.
   The trail lost, he looked about

   and shuffled forth, dry in mouth,
   aching for home and green remorro.
   In desert wastes the soul cries out

   in blind canyons, under blank sky. Scouting
   for water, throat parched and sore,
   with the trail lost he looked about
   desert wastes. The soul cries out.

2. "Come eat peyote and you shall live."
   The woman waved and called him on.
   "A god has made this road a gift."

   She crossed the arroyo and came to him
   cloaked in light and shakes of rain.
   "Come, eat peyote and you shall live."

   Her fingers brushed his blistered lips.
   She talked like water; touched like dawn.
   A god had made the road a gift.

   for in that realm of scorpion and snake
   his soul cried out and the woman came
   fashioned from light and veiled in rain.
   He followed a god through desert wastes.

PART TWO

Kate and Gary's Bar,
Red River, New Mexico

Just over the mountains from Eagle Nest
where the glacial maw ground out a valley
and oceans of gold aspens surge around steep
boulder fields and islands of evergreens and
the collapsing ghost town where hippies hole up
you come to Red River: a string of bars
and curio shops, all pine planks and logs.
The river rattles rocks behind the town.
Farther on, towards Questa where the Rockies open
to volcanic plains, a huge gray slag heap
slides towards the river from the molybdenum mine.
The town makes no claim on eternity,
a mere moment in the granite gorge
shadowed by whistling crags and forests
beside a river carving out canyons
eating its way to the sea.

Kate's son drove me into town,
picked me up off the road from Questa,
so I had her roast beef special and a beer.
She pulled a chair from the edge of the dance floor,
watched my Adam's apple bob with beer and studied
my backpack and sleeping bag leaning by the door.
"What do you do, anyway?" she asked. "You're no drifter."
"I write poetry," I said. She smiled,

and pushed her bifocals back up her nose.
"I knew you did something like that.
Grace," she called behind the bar
to the long-legged girl setting up drinks,
"bring our friend another Coors."

Tavern by a Mountain Stream

Legs crossed, I look out on the valley,
its paths winding towards a deserted tavern
thatch roof tattered and decayed.
Bamboo poles, laid down on gnarled pylons
and lashed together at creaky joints,
bridge the emerald stream uncurling
long grasses in the wavering current.
Happy, I forget my old worries.
Someone's kite is angling high above.

from the Vietnamese of Ho Xuan Huong

Eliseo's Cabin, Taos Pueblo

Yellow alfalfa banks the rutted lane
that winds in under the bedstead gate
latched with loops of baling wire.
Horse-skulls bleach on fenceposts
running down through sagebrush
to the cabin snug by the sandy creek.
Pieces of plows hang from the cedars
along with barn hinges, tractor chains,
and a rusted-out kettle. A buffalo hide
drapes a lodge pole wedged in willows.
The cabin's covered in sweetpea vines,
blossoms tumbling out bees.
Eliseo has set his cot outside
near an iron pot brimming peonies.

Lying alone at night, watching
stars shake, hearing the creek talk,
he remembers before there was a camp
and his father would come here to watch
thunderheads collapse on the prairie
and drag sweeps of rain across arroyos.
Worried about the old man sleeping on the ground

he sawed planks and hauled them up by buckboard
rocking to the meadow on wheels that smelled of sage.

Now old himself he comes to his cabin
to heat chili and bread on the wood stove
to sleep by the creek or sit by a spruce
whittling birds for grandchildren.
In the dark, he hears his ponies graze
across the fern-crowded creek
where fireflies flare like memories
and his father and grandchildren's voices
rise from the cold traveling water.

Spring-Watching Pavilion

A gentle spring evening arrives
airily, unclouded by worldly dust.
Three times the bell tolls echoes like a wave.
We see heaven upside down in sad puddles.
Love's vast sea cannot be emptied.
And springs of grace flow easily everywhere.
Where is nirvana?
Nirvana is here, nine times out of ten.

from the Vietnamese of Ho Xuan Huong

For John Haag, Logger, Sailor, Housepainter, Poet, Professor, and Grower of Orchids

---

This is between you and me, Haag.
In this College of Glooms
you saunter about in leather pants
pacing the halls as if they were a deck
from your sailing days in the Merchant Marine

. . .as if you were here on shore leave
and had to make ship in Seattle
tonight. . .tailing trucks through snowy foothills
as flurries veer at your windshield
and brake lights blink ahead on the turns
as you chant to yourself and the snow
all the poems you ever learned alone
on moon-washed nights when waves were listening:
Dylan Thomas. Wallace Stevens.
"The Astabula Bridge Disaster."
. . .yes, squinting into the dark and saying poems,
passing a truck on the straightaway
driving hard until you hit Puget Sound
where the sea rushes the rocks on the beach

under a fat moon wreathed in fog
and the bellbuoy chimes all night.

This is between the two of us, not
those who speculate, but never make;
who lodge in our mansion in rented rooms
and have tacked old carpets down
over all the holes in the floors. They
shall never mount the stairway of surprise
which angels showed us
unless we are their guides
up to the belfry where the sea is crashing
and the bell rings waves of light.

Daddy's Acting Odd in Springtime

March 1: Hopes Poke Through Furiously

Patches of snow in hollows. Bits of green on banks.
Through a mat of dry stalks, sheaves
of gilly flower, nettle, and burdock
shove into sunlight and uncurl. Now,
when the ground might freeze and heave up
or snow squall in from cold blue mountains,
he worries for these tender weeds.

March 15: Midnight Forest

Springs fork out through hillside stones
plunking into little pools wavering with duckweed.
Trickles collect into a creek
seeping through a dead hemlock bole
where the clear pan, straddled by roots,
ripples up a sliver moon and Jupiter's bright dot.

A fingerling circles this pool like a thought.

High overhead, Canada geese are honking home
spilling mad calls into cold air.

March 16: Throughout Rocking Trees

groaning on each other in windy woods
frozen by last night's rain, twigs and bark
enameled in ice, the fat buds strain.
Oh, such complaints, such a strew of ice-clatter
as cold limbs creak in blowing fog.

The oak's heart is hard, but runs to its taproot.
Where the maple is chafed, it bleeds sweet sap.

What's Papa up to? Is he lost?
He's twined a willow sprig around his head
and is laughing at arguing trees.

Let Him Be

Let the man be who had nothing to tell you,
let him mumble his beard over his mug of gall,
let him work his bread into bits at the table.
Let him think he's coughing because the tobacco's damp.

And let him, as he leaves, nod goodbye to the bottle
and go outside and leap from the porch into the night
and stride across the fields already thick with clover
to wave down the first truck that finds him in its lights.

Let him tell the wicked driver all about his ulcer,
how it keeps him up, hungry at odd times,
and how bread is not enough, no, not by bread alone
despite whatever may be the common thought.

Let him get off at a hill and go up to a pear tree
and punch his fist right through the twisted trunk,
clean through to the night, and, as the tree listens,
let him curse it in pain and shame and bitter hurt.

Because, life picks us up like little chunks of ryebread
and wads and works us in its rough, sweaty fist.
So let him be, this man who's walking down the hillside.
Let him alone. Let him slam the table with his fist.

from the Bulgarian of Georgi Borisov

57

Mountain

The mountain is there when you walk to Safeway.
The mountain is there when you leave the bank.
You can stare at the peaks all day,
at the juniper slopes piled up from the prairie,
the scree above the tree line.
Look all you want, it won't look back
although pickups poking along Santa Fe road
seem magnetized in the mountain's gaze.
Long searching looks and no replies.
Our world, seen through the 20th century squint.
The mountain's no symbol; merely there
though the Tiwas say it's sacred
and built their pueblo at its base,
watering their ponies in Blue Lake Creek,
adding adobe rooms through the thousand years.

At 4:00 A.M. Asleep

I wanted to shoot the jerk
whining his wheels on an ice patch
dragging me from sleep
even before sparrows screech the dawn
up from snow-crusted choirs of forsythia
between houses somehow asleep.
But maybe the jerk is a her not a him
some poor drudge who's finally had it
after a long night of shouts and slaps.

Maybe this suburb isn't the dead zone.
Maybe others are awake...some old guy
sitting up with arthritis, chain-smoking,
or a mother, leaning over a crib
stroking her child crackling with phlegm,
or some man fishing in a toilet bowl
as his wife sobs into her hands and he spoons up
the blood clot, the embryo sac, to take to the doctor
to see what went wrong.
                              Thinking these things
before falling back to sleep, I realized
I was called out into a field of compassion
into a universe of billions of souls, and
that was a messenger now driving away.

For My Sister in
Warminster General Hospital

The two birds augured something strange.
First, I saved the blackpoll warbler
that piped twice as the cat pounced
and clawed the slapping wings.
No blood, but the bird couldn't fly,
It pecked my warm hands.
Slept the night in a bamboo creel.
When I took it out the next morning
it peeped before bounding to a hemlock,
cocked its head at me,
and then flew off to Argentina.

Then the junco sitting by the door.
I scooped it up, making my hands a nest.
When I let it loose later in the day
it bobbed away in the little arcs
that juncos make from bush to bush.
Two birds in the same day. Just exhausted.

I've heard of whole migrations blown off course,
looking for the Orkneys, lost in the Atlantic,
plummeting like hail onto a passing ship
where they flopped, faltered, and died.
All about, birds falling into swells.

So these auguries were for you, my sister,
asthmatic, gasping to flex your lungs
for ten days, or so I learned tonight.

When I was small and could not breathe
you read me comics: Little Lulu and Scrooge McDuck
were our favorites. You read or made them up
while your skinny brother sat like a board in bed
and wheezed and panic widened in his eyes.

But I rested and flew off.
Thirty years later, you force your lungs for air.
Consider: whole flocks lost and blown into the sea.
Consider the sailors looking from that deck,
watching the waves engulf the keening birds.
It makes no sense; it only happens.

You be the bird that fell down exhausted,
that rested and took off, a bit later in the day.

A Woman Alone on the Road

It's a risk and a bother
in this world that's still male
when around each bend may lie
ambushes of absurd encounters
and the streets fix her
with cold stares.
This woman alone on the road.
Her only defense
is her defenselessness.

She hasn't made from any man
a crutch, or wayside shelter.
She never walked over a man
as if he were a bridge.
She went off alone
to meet him as an equal
and to love him truly.

Whether she'll go far
or falter in the mud
or be blinded by horizons
she doesn't know. She's stubborn.
Even if rebuked along the way
her setting out itself

is accomplishment enough.
A woman alone on the road.
And yet she goes on
and does not stop.

No man can be as lonesome
as a woman on her own.
Before her the darkness
drops down a locked door.
A woman alone on the road
ought not go out at night.
The dawn sun, like a turnkey,
will unlock her horizons.

Still she goes on
even in the darkness
not glancing about in fear
but each step measuring her faith
in the Dark Man
with whom she's been threatened
for a long time.
Her steps echo on the paving
and stub against a stone.
A woman alone on the road:
quiet brave steps over a sad earth,
an earth which, against the stars,
is a woman alone on the road.

from the Bulgarian of Blaga Dimitrova

South of L.A.

wet-suited surfers scud the green combers
and the freeway whines like a wire
here at San Onofre where reactor domes
hump up between sandcliffs and sea
and youngsters promenade the beach
in permed hair and sleekest tans
hoping like hell, for hell is just that:
not to be cast away, to be loved.

As egrets stalk the fouled lagoon
a coot clacks its beak in dry reeds
and, overhead, Camp Pendleton choppers,
Hueys and sleek Cobra gunships,
sweep dragonfly wings in churns of light.

I guess we know this all might blow,
that marsh and egrets, crabs and coots,
tanned teenagers and shimmering shoreline
could be no more than mulch and ash,
atomic smog just drifting out to sea,
drifting past the distant fog bank,
filtering down to the mid-Pacific ridge
that cooks up life in volcanic vents — that
someday our cells may chug through those shafts.

Estuary

They walked the footpath to the bay
where waves rinsed the pebbled shore
sloshing cedar roots and sedgey weeds.
Took off their shoes to wade
ankle-deep in cold salt water.
Minnows winked across their toes.
The woman tucked her skirt above her knees
and he slung his coat across his back
as they wandered along without talking
as, farther out, gulls rocked on the tide.
They searched the water slowly
as if it were their hearts and now
and then they bent to lift a stone or shell,
showing them to each other, smiling
as though each had found some wondrous thing.
He found a stone as coral as her lips
and then two tiny spiralled shells, white
and whorled in long perfect turrets.
You never find them whole, he said
And here were two so close together.

Autumn Landscape

Drop by drop rain slaps the banana leaves.
Praise whomever's skill sketched this desolate scene:
the lush, dark canopies of the gnarled trees;
the long river, sliding smooth and white.
Tilting my wine flask, I am drunk with rivers and hills.
My bag, filled with wind and moonlight, weighs on my back,
sags with poems. Look, and love even men.
Whoever sees this landscape is stunned.

from the Vietnamese of Ho Xuan Huong

Deer Kill

The deer was down in a bed of maple leaves,
leaves dappled red, like blood, in the evening.
Grabbed the spindly hocks and heaved, rolling
the heavy doe on her back. Her eyes still clear.

Cut through the leaking web of nipples,
opening the belly like a burlap sack.
The blade's razor edge nicked her stomach bag
venting a stink of fermenting grass.

Freed the livid sheath from the red walls.
Her blood pumped out. From a severed tube.
In a scalding pool. In the great rib cage.
Heart, fatter than a hand, soapy to touch.

Pink rags of huge, shattered lungs.
Dropped liver out onto scratchy leaves.
Shook loose her stomach, bladder, and bowels.
Cleaved the pelvic ring with an ax.

Hand in the clean womb of the doe,
wet and white like chicken fat.

Threw a fist of it across the stream
rilling over stones under the chill moonlight.
Dabbed leaves in blood and stuck them to my face.
Screamed "wolf" at the moon; moon said, "man."

Walking Down into Cebolla Canyon

Then, truly unhappy, terrified by Fate, wearied by the empty sky,
Dido prayed for death.
  —AENEID, BOOK IV 450

1. Everything about us, for better or worse,
   we make ourselves, with marvelous exceptions:
   The snow peaks rinsed in rose light
   at dusk on the Sangre de Cristo range.
   The bleached, broken jaw of a mule deer,
   its teeth scattered among cactus wreaths
   beside the trail, down from the mesa,
   where the river stammers against volcanic
   rocks and pools where spooked trout skim
   through aspen leaves tumbling in clear water.

2. The river cut through centuries of rock
   to this time when all assertions are suspect,
   to this century when assurances are mute,
   when we, deserted like Dido before her pyre
   or Raleigh pacing The Lie in the Tower,
   look up to see "a wearying, empty sky,"
   and gag on words like sour meats
   stewed in the stomach of a haggis sheep.
   So, pity the poets, whose work is words,
   reduced to blather or fiery silences
   when God who breathed the Word expired.

3. This vast rubble offers its one blessing:
   everything it says is true – parched mesa,
   willow water, fox skull, circling raven,
   tarantula, deer turd, singing wren.
   One wanders down past living metaphors,
   Where life is threatened, no lies are told.
   Under a blank sky one clambers past
   collapsed ledges clustered with paintbrush
   blue saxifrage and hooded columbine.
   Small. Alone. No better than a bug.

4. If one accepts these terms, he takes his place
   offered all along by the ribboned stream
   calling up from the bouldered canyon floor,
   to stand here at dusk and stare at spilling water
   near a wren jigging on a laved slab
   in the river which leaps through lunar wastes
   where trout, coyote, magpie, cougar, prosper
   in the innocence which humans find in love.
   Child, I bring back the water's benediction:

   "The streams we play in flow sweet water.
   Anyone might drink here and be refreshed.
   All day, sunlight strikes the river clear,
   At dusk, the current ripples with a moon.
   Love like water makes the canyons bloom."

Flying Home

(For Tally, Age Three)

So this is how the journey ends.
I'm sitting here in a Lottaburger
near Winchell's Donut, in Albuquerque
across the street from Miniature Golf
where a teen in tight jeans and Danskin top
twirls a putter, majorette-style.

Just over there is the 7-11,
while over here, an Exxon and Skat.
Above the Sandias a thunderstorm
drops thunderbolts and drags the rain.
A wayward bird careens in sight,
blown by gusts and flapping wildly.

In two more days I fly back home.
When I scoop you up into a hug
you'll cry, "Don't crush me *bones!*"
My tiny guide to a wiser life.
Little wren who calls me home.

John Balaban is Professor of English and MFA Director at Penn State and author of six books of fiction and poetry, including *After Our War* which won the Lamont Selection of the Academy of American Poets and a nomination for the National Book Award. In Spring, 1991, Poseidon/Simon and Schuster will publish his memoir, *Remembering Heaven's Face. Words for My Daughter* is his third book of poetry.